THE AUTHORITY OF SCRIPTURE

A SPURGEON'S BOOKLET

The Authority of Scripture

ANDREW RIGDEN GREEN

KINGSWAY PUBLICATIONS
EASTBOURNE

First published 1990

Cover design by Ron Bryant-Funnell

British Library Cataloguing in Publication Data

Green, Andrew Rigden
The authority of scripture.
1. Bible. Authority
I. Title
220'.1'3

ISBN 0–86065–806–6

Printed in Great Britain for
KINGSWAY PUBLICATIONS LTD
1 St Anne's Road, Eastbourne, E Sussex BN21 3UN by
Richard Clay Ltd, Bungay, Suffolk
Typeset by Watermark, Hampermill Cottage, Watford

Contents

Preface

Founded in 1856 by the Victorian 'Prince of Preachers', Charles Haddon Spurgeon, Spurgeon's College is an evangelical Baptist theological college located in south London, which over the years has trained many hundreds of men and women for Christian leadership both in the UK and overseas. Spurgeon's has always had a strong emphasis on vocational as well as academic training. It is only natural therefore that, in association with Kingsway Publications, Spurgeon's, under its Principal Paul Beasley-Murray, has teamed up to produce this present series of booklets, which aim to cover a wide variety of pastoral issues.

Before becoming Principal of Spurgeon's in 1986, Paul Beasley-Murray served with the Baptist Missionary Society in Zaïre (1970–72) and for thirteen years was Pastor of the Baptist Church in Altrincham, Cheshire (1973–1986).

1

The Authority of Scripture

The source of authority

When asked to defend the authority of the Bible, Charles H Spurgeon retorted, 'You don't need to defend a lion, just let it out of its cage.' So the subject of this booklet might seem unnecessary and incongruous to him.

However, we live in a sceptical age in which few things are taken as self-evident, least of all those things labelled as Authorities. Every human authority claims a higher authority to justify itself. So, like Theseus, we need to trace the skein of thread out of the labyrinth to its very source. Moreover, we should not be ashamed of our task. Despite Spurgeon's comment, this task of searching out a basis for authority is an honourable one. Jesus discussed at great length the basis of his authority (Jn 5) and then performed miracles 'that you may know that the Son of Man has authority' (Mt 9:6). Jesus was quite happy to let everyone know that his ultimate authority derived from God.

This is where we begin. If God is the *principium essendi*, the first cause in theology, then he is the locus for all life and knowledge, all power and authority. There is no further authority to which we can appeal; and he is his own authority because there is nothing greater outside himself.

Characteristics of authority

Starting with God like this enables us to define authority and see its main characteristics. At the heart of the Christian idea of God there is the implicit assumption that he can put into action whatever he wills. To put any limits to his power would be to deny his deity. Thus, in his relation to men, he has the right to command obedience. This power to act and this right to obedience is his authority.

It is noteworthy, therefore, that in the English New Testament the words 'power', 'right' and 'authority' are all interchangeable translations for the Greek word *exousia* (eg, Mt 7:29, 8:9, 9:6; Jn 1:12, 5:27, 17:2). In whatever context we examine authority – whether it is the police, the state, the Bible or God – there is always this sense that there is a power or right to command obedience.

Since all authority ultimately derives from God, we can go on to say that authority can be delegated. Usually this is an authority bestowed upon another so that there is a chain of authority from the higher to the lower. Thus the Crown gives authority to the Lord Chancellor, and the Lord Chancellor gives authority to the judges. In this country all civil, judicial and military power can trace a line of authority to the Crown, which in turn finds its authority in God. This is bestowed authority.

A second form of authority is not bestowed from above, but inherent in itself. Thus Jesus showed that he had both forms of authority. God had bestowed upon him an authority from above (Jn 5; Mt 28:18), but he also had an authority in himself (Mt 7:29). In other words, as the submissive Son he was obedient to the Father and received authority from him; but as the Word of God made flesh he had authority in himself. The authority of the Son is therefore the authority of the Father: the two work hand in hand (Jn 5:17, 19, 22, etc). To have seen the Son is to have seen the Father. To have heard the Son is to have heard God's words. This is a crucial point in any Christian argument concerning authority. Jesus is the Word of God, and in him all God's authority resides.

To posit all ultimate authority in Jesus, the Word of God, is a basic axiom. It is a base camp from which we can climb higher – though some guides to authority will point out different routes further up the mountain. What is most significant, however, is that this base camp is a place where many fellow travellers meet. Liberals and catholics rub shoulders with evangelicals. For this reason it is important to pause here and explore the terrain of common ground.

Authority and faith in Christ

When we speak about faith in Christ, we are expressing not only the central object of our worship – Jesus Christ – but also something of the means of understanding that object – through faith. If we examine this centre of belief we will come closer to understanding the foundations of authority. There are at least three ways in which faith in Christ relates to authority.

1. By understanding the importance of faith in Christ, the propriety of faith in any question of authority is revealed

To believe that Christ is the eternal Word of God is an article of faith as much as it is to say that God created the world out of nothing. No amount of logic can prove this authority by pure reason. Yet millions of people – academic and non-academic, clergy and lay-people – are happy to see their ultimate authority decided by faith. As we shall see, this does not mean that faith is the opposite of reason or that it necessitates a blind leap in the dark.

The point is simply that faith is a vital part of our understanding of authority.

2. Faith in Christ breaks any circularity of argument

Since Scripture provides the primary source for our understanding of Jesus, there may seem to be a problem in our methodology of understanding (epistemology). There seems to be a circle which goes like this: 'We believe in Jesus because we believe what the Bible says about Jesus; and we believe the Bible because of what Jesus says about the Bible.'

In fact the circle of such an argument is broken by faith. This faith is not an irrational step or the result of some mystical experience. A combination of data work together to inform the mind, direct the will and sensitise the spirit. Scripture, tradition, reason and experience are taken by the Holy Spirit to impress upon us the truth of Christ. It is impossible to speak of authority in a Christian context without recognising the priority of this work of the Spirit which brings faith in Christ. This work of the Spirit is both a fundamental doctrine and an essential experience, whatever our ecclesiastical tag.

3. Faith in the person Jesus Christ is intrinsically tied to a commitment to his authority as Lord

Indeed, the declaration 'Jesus is Lord' is the earliest Christian creed. A Christian who makes this confession will therefore seek to align his life with the teaching and life of Christ. Thus the attitude of Jesus to Scripture and authority is not of secondary importance; rather it goes to the very heart of Christian discipleship. Our attitude to Scripture impinges directly upon faith in Christ.

Authority and the incarnation of Christ

There is a very close link between the doctrine of Scripture and incarnation. The main point of contact between a doctrine of incarnation and Scripture concerns transcendence and immanence. At the heart of the Christian message is the good news that God is with us in Christ; the transcendent God is immanent in the affairs of men. John says, 'The Word was made flesh.' In Jesus we see both God and man, two natures in one Person, revealed in space and time. To understand Christ both natures have to be taken seriously: he is not half God and half man, but fully God and fully man.

Similarly, the Scriptures are both divine and human. The divine message is recorded by human beings, but the Scriptures remain one. In the Bible the transcendent God reveals himself and is immanent in that which is human. Clearly the analogy cannot be taken too far for Jesus is ontologically one with the Father, the creator and redeemer. Scripture, on the other hand, is distinct from and apart from God. The Bible is a creaturely instrument of God, not God in person. Despite these distinctions the doctrine of incarnation sheds light on our understanding of Scripture. We cannot make an *a priori* assumption that God cannot reveal himself through humanity. We cannot automatically assume that all things human are full of error and sin. The incarnation opens our eyes to what God can do through frail human flesh. If God could work his perfect purpose in Christ, he can also do this in Scripture. This leads us to questions about language, culture and human understanding.

The realm of language

It is suggested by some that truth cannot be communicated by ordinary language because human words are finite and imprecise. Now there can be no doubt that for God to use human language he must accommodate himself to man. The point, however, is this: if God could accommodate himself to the speech of Jesus, then he can accommodate himself to the writing of Scripture.

The realm of culture

A doctrine of Scripture and incarnation both recognise an accommodation to culture. Jesus was a man who spoke within the conceptual framework of a culture that was bound by time. Nevertheless, although speaking within the limitations of a culture, Jesus spoke timeless truth. So one can argue that the cultural horizons of Scripture do not raise impossible obstacles to understanding. They need to be understood and taken into account; but Scripture can still speak into other cultures and at other ages with timeless truth.

The realm of human perception

Clearly the significance of the person and work of Christ was understood according to the perspective of the observers of the time. For example the Pharisees saw Jesus in a different light from that of John's disciples. Nevertheless, despite a different perception of the significance of Jesus' ministry, the actual meaning of his incarnation remains the same for all people in all time. This is God with us and revealed to us. Perceptions of significance may vary and be quite subjective, but meaning has an objectivity.

Thus, when we come to study Scripture the problems of interpretation need careful evaluation. This need not mean, however, that we drown in a sea of subjectivity. The incarnation is an anchor in time and space; human perception cannot rob it of its objective reality.

The mystery of God's condescension to us in the Scriptures has to have links with God's condescension to us in Christ. For all sorts of reasons – cultural, literary, emotional – we find it difficult to comprehend that the infinite and eternal should communicate through that which is finite and bound by time. But this is how God has revealed himself to us in Christ; so we can assume that he does the same thing in Scripture.

One authority above others

Our search for a basis for authority has already made us aware of the interrelation of tradition, reason and Scripture. Richard Hooker (1554–1600) drew attention to these three sources of authority in the sixteenth century. To say which source of authority has priority over the others, and the relationship between all three, is an issue as much alive in our day as it was in the days of Hooker. Yet something must be said about these authorities before we can proceed any further.

1. No one authority can be taken in isolation

If Scripture has no relation with tradition or reason then it is at the mercy of private evaluation and individual flights of fancy. Much of the fragmentation of Protestant sects is witness to this sad fact. Alternatively, when reason is the sole authority, subjectivism is the order of the day. Thus some liberal churches have lost all anchor in biblical and historic Christianity. Thirdly, the Catholic church, giving priority to tradition, has sometimes worked against Scripture and excluded private judgement, thus shackling the intellect and will.

If we cannot, therefore, take one source of authority in complete isolation, can we place them in some sort of relation to one another? Clearly this has been done in the past. Each branch of Christian tradition represented in denominations and parties has a priority given to one authority above the other. Rather like building-blocks each authority is set in a different order. When we add other components like experience and conscience, the permutations of order among the building-blocks become more complex. Nevertheless, we can say that generally, Catholics have put the emphasis on tradition, liberals on reason and evangelicals on Scripture.

2. Scripture is at the apex of any pyramid of authorities

For evangelicals, Scripture's supreme place among other authorities centres on its unique relationship to God and his Christ – who are ultimate authorities. Human tradition and human reason by definition originate with man and his world. Scripture, on the other hand, says that it originates from God as he breathes it out.. Although Scripture is an instrument of God, it claims a delegated authority as God's words to man. If this divine origin can be substantiated, then we have an authority that is above all others. The rest of this booklet is an attempt at substantiating that Scripture is in fact God-breathed; and as such it is our supreme authority.

2

Revelation

So far we have established that all authority is in God and in his Christ. As the Word of God, Jesus Christ is God's unique revelation to man. Whether or not the Bible can also be called 'the word of God' and whether it presents propositional truth in an objective form is a matter we must now discuss.

Much of the debate revolves around the idea of whether God can or cannot reveal himself. We shall look at three different attitudes to revelation and Scripture, each roughly corresponding to the liberal, neo-orthodox and evangelical positions. As though in dialogue we shall take the latter point of view and let the other positions argue against it. Although we have yet to clarify terms, we need to know what we mean by an evangelical position. Historically evangelicals have upheld the authority of Scripture as the word of God. They argue that the Bible represents God's words in an objective, propositional, written form that is reliable and true. As we state the arguments against this position we shall find that the encounter with other views is not a sterile exercise: rather, the interaction with differing views sharpens our understanding of the nature of authority.

The liberal position: the Bible is not the word of God, but merely the testimony of men

Classic liberal theology stems largely from the thinking of Immanuel Kant (1724–1804) and Friedrich Schleiermacher (1768–1834). Both looked at the being of God and man (ontology) and also the way we go about knowing things (epistemology). Kant, influenced by the Enlightenment, said that because we are finite beings our knowledge is limited to the world of man's perceptions – 'the phenomenal world'. He reconstructed religion on the basis of man's inner sense of duty. Schleiermacher saw this philosophy as a basis for his theology so that man's inner conscience became his authority and the foundation for his understanding of God. These eighteenth and nineteenth-century thinkers were also writing at a time when principles of literary criticism were being applied to the Bible and to them it seemed that the Bible was full of legends and errors. Thus, on the basis of these suppositions, it appeared that the Bible could not be the word of God. They argued that the finite cannot know the infinite; and that records purporting to be 'revelation' were manifestly human, not divine.

Kant and Schleiermacher represent a watershed in biblical and theological studies. Those following their course had to find a new basis of authority. As we look back over more than a century of liberal thinking, the authority of Scripture as the objective word of God has always been subtly denied. It is important to understand the arguments employed. They have said:

1. The Bible cannot be the objective word because the word is dynamic

Thus many theologians see the Bible as primarily a

record of salvation history. As the story of salvation unfolds, so previously understood principles concerning God may be corrected and even contradicted; but such inconsistencies in the record do not matter. God cannot be understood in a static and unchanging book, because God himself is not static. A dynamic God reveals himself in his activity in history.

This emphasis on dynamic revelation is a helpful corrective to static models of biblical revelation. Nevertheless, a dynamic approach is not incompatible with an understanding of the Bible as the objective word of God. It should not be assumed that an historic event which is given specific meaning through Scripture (like the Passover) could not have a wider application than in that particular time in history. Clearly, there is a dynamic progression of revelation in Scripture; not that later truth corrects earlier truth – but that further revelation 'fills out' what has gone before.

2. *The Bible cannot be the objective word because we encounter God existentially*

An existential encounter with God is an obvious way out of the liberal impasse of authority. If there is no final authority in Scripture, tradition or reason, then that personal encounter with God can become one's supreme guide. If one is committed to this existential view of revelation then any suggestion that the Bible presents objective propositional truth is anathema. Truth does not come in a detached or neutral form. When God speaks to people it is person to person.

This sense of encounter with God in Scripture, for which Rudolf Bultmann (1884–1976) and others argue, is entirely right and proper. For example, Jesus' parables force the hearer to make a decision and a commitment. It is not enough merely to listen to Jesus; one must encounter him and act on his words. Thus, any orthodoxy which omits this existential factor is sadly lacking. Nevertheless, Bultmann's approach is inadequate in that it assumes something is true only when there has been personal response and encounter. The fact, however, that we do not respond does not invalidate truth. My wife exists whether or not I want to encounter and respond to her! Thus to deny Scripture that sense of objective truth simply because there may be no existential encounter is to go too far.

The argument is inadequate.

3. The Bible cannot be the word of God because it is time-bound and inaccurate

The basic phenomenon of the Bible, viewed as a purely human piece of literature, has always been a prime argument against accepting the authority of Scripture. Just one aspect of this question is the time-bound thought forms of every culture and age. This is a problem which theologians like Bultmann and J.A.T. Robinson have tried to tackle by their programme of demythologising. Their basic assumption has been that each culture in history has had its own way of expressing truth, whether it is in terms of mythological or philosophical paradigms. Robinson comments: 'These are simply different ways of representing reality; we must choose whatever one means most to us.'[1]

Dennis Nineham puts the problem even more directly: 'To believe in the halting of the sun, or for that matter the raising of Lazarus from the dead, is to hold to quite a different belief from that which was held by the biblical writers.'[2] He goes on: 'In the light of modern understanding of the physical universe as an interlocking system, a miracle would entail an exercise of divine power on a far greater scale than previous periods envisaged.'[3] Now, Nineham is not dealing with the question of whether it is possible to believe in miracles in the twentieth century. He is raising the more simple issue: just that we know more science than they did 2,000 years ago. But what difference does this make? At the tomb of Lazarus, Mary knew nothing of the cellular nature of body tissue and the physiological damage brought by death. Nevertheless, whether it is the first or the twenty-first century, the miracle is the same! Undoubtedly the Bible is not written in scientific terminology, and its observations of nature are couched in terms appropriate for that age. These are not, however, inaccuracies as such and do not undermine the Bible's implicit claim to be the word of God in every age.

This liberal position has many disciples today and takes many forms. Yet the head of this stream of thinking is still Kant and the Enlightenment. It was an age that dethroned God and in his place put man's reason as authority. Consequently, much liberal theology is not so much an explanation of God as an exploration of the mind of man. What began as a quest for more certain knowledge sank into a mire of subjectivity. In direct reaction to this, Karl Barth suggested a new approach, and to this we now turn.

The neo-orthodox position: the Bible 'contains' the word of God

The bankruptcy of liberalism has been apparent to many, but the break with liberalism was never more dramatic or more significant than in the life and writing of Karl Barth (1886–1968). The son of a pastor, Barth was nurtured on liberalism but found that it led nowhere. As he turned to Scripture, he rediscovered within it the word of God. Barth's theology has been tremendously positive and influential. The Neo-orthodox revolution which he initiated has brought about a recovery of the importance of the authority of Scripture. However, the basic suppositions of this position need to be examined. So often he is correct in what he affirms, but unhelpful in what he denies.

1. The Bible only 'contains' the word of God because God is transcendent

Barth's greatest criticism of liberalism was the way God was being made in the image of man. Barth's theology rightly emphasised God as the transcendent being wholly unlimited by the finitude of man. The implication of this position for Barth was that if God was 'wholly other', then neither his person nor his truth could be limited to mere words. The Bible writers had a clear revelatory experience of God but what they wrote is not propositional truth, just a human account of their experience. Within this very human revelation we can encounter the word of God, but the Bible is not in itself the objective word of God. Of course, Barth's desire to let God be God is entirely laudable, but in his efforts to preserve the sovereignty of God, he has moved liberalism back into the sort of subjectivity he so sorely disliked in liberalism.

2. The Bible only 'contains' the word of God because God gives himself, not propositions

Barth's subjectivity is further illustrated by his insistence that Scripture is only the word of God as it *becomes* the word in existential encounter as the Holy Spirit works on Scripture. Barth said that the knowledge of God is ontologically objective but epistemologically subjective. The reason for this subjectivity is that the sovereign God must not be tied to what he describes as a worldly document. However, we must ask, does our knowledge of something always imply a mastery of that thing? The fact that God binds himself by covenant to his people does not make him less like God. So one can argue that God's unique self-disclosure does not tie him down.

3. The Bible only 'contains' the word of God because the truth of Scripture demands a priori *faith*

G C Berkouwer, who has been much influenced by Barth, argues that it is impossible to speak of objective truth in Scripture because truth needs an *a priori* commitment of faith. Berkouwer caricatures an evangelical approach to Scripture when he says it is 'An incorrect conception of theology, a conception which considers it possible to discern Holy Scripture apart from a personal relationship of belief in it as though that alone would constitute *objectivity*.'[4] This is another aspect of the existential argument which has value in that God's truth does make demands. Indeed, this is at the core of our understanding of authority: the power or right to command obedience. Nevertheless, the fact that an authority is disobeyed or ignored does not diminish the objective reality of that authority. Thus Scripture's authority and objectivity is diminished neither because there is no *a priori* faith, nor because there is no obedience following.

The evangelical position: the Bible is the word of God

The evangelical view of Scripture is that although the Bible is written by human beings, it is at the same time the word of God. This word has an objective reality regardless of man's attitude to it or his cultural vantage point. It presents propositional truth to man in every age.

This assertion needs a justification that is sympathetic to the contemporary debate on Scripture. All too often positions become needlessly polarised as though liberal, neo-orthodox or evangelical parties have nothing to learn from one another. In fact most criticisms have a kernel of truth that is worth hearing. The four dangers outlined here represent pitfalls for Christians of every party or none! By being sensitive to the dialogue on each side of the debate, the evangelical position can be better understood.

1. The danger of false antithesis and over-simplification

One of the chief dangers of polarised positions is the problem of false antithesis. Both liberal and neo-orthodox positions argue against the evangelical insistence on objective propositional truth found in Scripture. For them this evangelical position seems to be too static and mechanical. It appears to give to Scripture a power independent of God's Spirit. Such a position, they argue, leads to a form of bibliolatry with a fourth member of the Godhead. Their comments are justified when some sects are examined. But historic evangelicalism has always insisted that God's revelation in Scripture is dependent on the dynamic of the Spirit. Moreover there is no dichotomy between that which is 'personal' and 'propositional'; for propositional truth to have personal effect there must be an existential encounter. For the same reason we must not set the statement 'the Bible *becomes* the word of God' against 'the Bible *is* the word of God'. The word of God has no personal impact unless, by the Spirit, it *becomes* in personal experience what it already is. That which is ontologically objective must become epistemologically subjective.

2. The danger of ignoring the phenomenon of the Bible

One of the chief arguments against taking the Bible as the word of God is its very form and content. Examined purely in literary terms, the Bible is made up of writings from many authors; sometimes a tradition is reused and reinterpreted so that questions of source and author are highly complex. Then if the Bible is examined from an historic or scientific background, the language is found to be imprecise and ambiguous. Critics of the evangelical position will say that the phenomenon of Scripture, taken at face value, demonstrates that the Bible cannot be the word of God. James Barr argues that Jesus alone can be called the Word of God and the Bible is just a testimony to him. He comments: 'It is wrong to say the Bible is revelation; it is witness to revelation.'[5] Barr would call the Bible the word only in a secondary sense.

The accusation against evangelicals is a serious one. First, there is the accusation that those who are supposed to take the Bible seriously do not in fact do so. Secondly, there is the accusation that evangelicals come with an *a priori* assumption concerning the nature of this revelation and thereby make more of Scripture than it is. Thirdly, because of in-built assumptions, evangelicals are accused of actually distorting the very text which they are supposed to revere.

Donald Carson summarises the central issues. First, do evangelicals who accept the claims of Scripture to truth also accept the phenomenon of Scripture? Secondly, granted that the Scriptures claim to be truthful, does the actual phenomenon of Scripture allow these high claims to stand? Behind both these issues is a question of either inductive or deductive methodology. In other words, do we make inductive conclusions about Scripture because we start with the phenomenon of the Bible? Alternatively, do we work deductively from the truth claims of the Bible and then in that light examine the phenomenon of Scripture? In fact, most thinking includes inductive and deductive reasoning as well as creative thought.[6] Roger Nicole gives illustrations of the way we normally think theologically. For example, as we consider Christ's relation to sin, do we start (inductively) with express statements concerning his sinlessness in Hebrews or do we begin (deductively) with the data about the life of Christ?[7] Clearly there is a relationship between the two methodologies. If by deduction we find the hard facts do not fit the hypothesis, then a new hypothesis must be made. But starting with an inductive hypothesis is not wrong methodology. This is a basic way of scientific investigation. Thus, what Scripture says about itself, and what Jesus says about Scripture, is of vital importance. When we have examined Scripture's own claim to truth we can come back to the phenomenon of the Bible and its inspiration.

3. The danger of ignoring truth claims of Scripture

A phenomenological approach to Scripture is in danger of ignoring Scripture's own testimony about itself. Although Scripture is made up of narrative and poetry as well as direct speech, Scripture regards all its witness as the 'word of God'. Psalm 119 speaks of all the law as God's 'word' despite the fact that most of it is historical narrative (Ps 119:9, 17, 25, etc). Similarly, the New Testament evaluates all of Scripture as the inspired word regardless of the type of literature (2 Tim 3:16; 2 Pet 1:20–21). This self-authentication may seem methodologically suspect, since we are used to authority having an external justification. However, Scripture has no higher authority to which it can appeal so it authenticates itself. The circularity of argument is broken as we examine Jesus' attitude to Scripture.

(I) WE MUST NOTE THAT JESUS SAW THE OLD TESTAMENT AS THE WORD OF GOD

He constantly referred to the Scriptures as vindicating his authority, saying, 'It is written' (Mt 4:4). In religious controversies, Jesus always used Scripture as the final arbiter (Mt 19:4). Indeed, Jesus never put himself above the Scriptures, saying, 'Heaven and earth would not disappear ... until everything is accomplished' (Mt 5:18). He saw that Scripture was written by the Holy Spirit and was not just the record of man (Lk 24:25). He accepted as accurate historical events (Mk 12:26; Lk 11:31), and he accepted Old Testament prophecy as God's word (Mt 11:10; Mk 7:6).

Of course, many theologians respond to this by saying that Jesus was accommodating his words to the prevailing intellectual and theological preconceptions of the time. Yet in so many ways Jesus cut across the thinking of his day. For example, in Matthew 6 Jesus is constantly criticising the traditions of his day by appealing to an authentic interpretation of Scripture, not to the prevailing understanding of his day. Indeed, since so much of Jesus' ministry was directed and governed by Old Testament Scripture, one must take his view seriously.

(II) WE MUST NOTE JESUS' VIEW OF HIS OWN WORDS

Clearly Jesus recognised that his words had unique authority. He said, 'The words I have spoken to you are spirit and they are life' (Jn 6:63); 'Whoever hears my word and believes him who sent me has eternal life' (Jn 5:24). More than this, Jesus believed his words would be eternally true: 'Heaven and earth will pass away, but my words will never pass away' (Mk 13:31).

(III) WE MUST NOTE JESUS' VIEW OF THE WORDS OF THE APOSTLES WHO FOLLOWED HIM

It is clear that Jesus had a strategy which involved the calling together of men endowed with the Spirit to teach in his name and with his authority (Mt 28:18; Jn 20:21; Acts 1:8). He also promised that the Holy Spirit would guide them into truth (Jn 14:26, 15:26, 16:13). Not surprisingly, therefore, we find that the Apostles claimed a direct experience of Christ's authority and insight (1 Cor 2:9, 10:3; Col 4:16). They also proclaimed the gospel confident that they spoke by the Holy Spirit (1 Cor 2:13; 2 Pet 1:21) and therefore used their apostolic teaching to judge the authenticity of all other teaching (1 Cor 14:37). Indeed, Peter actually lumps Paul's letters with 'the scriptures' (2 Pet 3:16).

4. The danger of ignoring reason and tradition and the inner witness

If the Scriptures really are the word of God, then we would expect the Bible to speak of itself as such. Moreover, one would expect the endorsement of the Word made flesh, Jesus Christ. There can be no higher authority to which to appeal! Nevertheless, since it is Scripture itself recording the words of Christ, it is its own self-authentication. Although there will never be a completely watertight system of justification, one might ask if there are other methods of justifying Scripture as the word of God.

(I) EXTERNAL JUSTIFICATION

John Locke (1632–1704) set up a framework for external justification to test whether something was a revelation from God. It was a revelation, he said, if: (a) it contained nothing inconsistent with what was evidently true; (b) when originally given the revelation was accompanied by impressive signs; (c) the account is historically true. Locke's work is important because he attempted to give reasons for revelation which were not entirely arbitrary or internal to Scripture itself. His argument was that if this revelation is true then one would expect its truth to be consistent with other truths upon which it touches. Thus Locke's thinking became a standard Protestant apologetic. B B Warfield said, 'Let it be proved that the true sense of some point of the original autograph is directly and necessarily inconsistent with some certainly known fact of history or truth of science.'[8] Thus the gauntlet is thrown down by Warfield and it is a legitimate challenge. If Scripture claims to be true, it should be seen to be true.

(II) INTERNAL JUSTIFICATION

Not only should Scripture be consistent with things outside itself, it should be internally consistent in order to justify itself as God's word. First, since we believe in a rational God, evidence of his mind should be seen in Scripture. Secondly, the moral content should be such that befits a righteous and holy God. Problems concerning the imprecatory Psalms, judgement and hell must be considered carefully. The exercise is fraught with difficulty, for how can poor finite sinners stand in judgement upon the moral and rational qualities of God? Nevertheless, this avenue of investigation cannot be ignored.

(III) THE JUSTIFICATION OF TRADITION

Tradition can in no sense justify a doctrine, but conversely if there is no tradition for a certain doctrine, then that doctrine must be suspect. Thus a sense of history can act as a brake on theological novelties. In order, therefore, to justify a doctrine of Scripture as the word of God, one would expect to see a tradition of this doctrine. Happily, church history provides a long line of theologians who have upheld the doctrine of Scripture as the word of God.

(IV) THE JUSTIFICATION OF AN INNER WITNESS OF THE SPIRIT

However hard we try to justify Scripture as the word of God, no methodology will provide watertight proof. Nevertheless many will speak of an existential authentication through the Spirit. Calvin put it like this: 'The highest proof of scripture derives from the fact that God in person speaks in it ... as God alone is a witness to himself in his Word, so also the Word will not find acceptance in men's hearts before it is sealed by the inward testimony of the Spirit.'[9]

The authoritative power of Scripture lies in its relation to God, who is the ground of all authority. It is our contention that Scripture is the word of God. Jesus Christ, the Word made flesh, makes this attestation to the authority of Scripture, as does Scripture itself. There are many tests that we can make as to the veracity of these claims – literary, historical and philosophical. Some of these questions will be tackled as we now think about the inspiration of Scripture.

Notes

1. J A T Robinson, *The Human Face of God* (SCM: London, 1974), p 195.
2. Dennis Nineham, *The Use and Abuse of the Bible* (SPCK: London, 1978), p 26.
3. *Ibid*, p 33.
4. G C Berkouwer, *Holy Scripture* (Eerdmans: Grand Rapids, MI, 1975), p 9.
5. J Barr, *The Bible in the Modern World* (SCM: London, 1977), p 28.
6. Donald Carson and John Woodbridge, eds, *Hermeneutics, Authority and Canon* (Inter Varsity Press: Leicester, 1986), p 23.
7. Roger Nicole, 'The Inspiration of Scripture: BB Warfield and Dr Dewey M Beagle', in *The Golden Review*, No 8 (1965–66). Quoted in Donald Carson and John Woodbridge, eds, *op cit*, p 106.
8. A A Hodge and B B Warfield, ed Roger Nicole, *Inspiration* (1979), p 36.
9. John Calvin, *Institutes of the Christian Religion*, Vol I, No vii, p 4.

3

Inspiration

Theories of inspiration

The Bible says that it is *theopneustos* – literally, God-breathed (2 Tim 3:16). Indeed, this term denotes something stronger than *in*spiration, for it should properly be translated as *ex*piration – that is, God breathing out. Paul's emphasis in 2 Timothy 3:16 is therefore entirely on divine activity in the production of Scripture. Peter, on the other hand, brings human and divine elements together, for he says Scripture came to be written because 'men moved by the Holy Spirit spoke from God' (2 Pet 1:21).

The Bible tells us no more about the mechanics of this divine and human combination. As with the incarnation, we are left with a profound mystery. Scripture is not half the work of man and half the work of God; rather, in the pages of Scripture we see something fully human and fully divine. Wrestling with this issue is important. For closely connected to the question of inspiration is the burning issue of reliability; and questions of reliability are connected to our major concern, that of authority. If the Bible has any authority – any right or power to command obedience – then it must be shown to be the work of men, reliably inspired by Almighty God.

As in the doctrine of Christ, the doctrine of Scripture has to tackle the mystery of the human and divine combined. Every Christological controversy has its origins in an unbalanced stress on one of the two natures of Christ. Docetism stressed the divine nature of Christ to the neglect of his human nature. Arianism did the reverse. Later, Apollinarianism and Nestorianism kept up the same swings of the pendulum. Now, the debate about Scripture revolves around the same issues. Using a coarse measure of categorisation, one can say there are four solutions to the problem.

1. The divine element is kept pure by dominating the human element

The so-called 'dictation theory' suggests that in the work of inspiration the divine element dominated the human. Thus the divine content of Scripture was communicated onto paper with no human contamination. The human authors, therefore, acted like mere dictating machines for the Lord. The advantage of this theory for its protagonists is that the divine authority of Scripture seems to be safeguarded. Ironically, however, this point of view does not take seriously the Bible's testimony to itself. Again and again Scripture gives credit to human authors who have clearly had some involvement in the process of inspiration. For example, 'holy men of God spake' (2 Pet 1:21, Authorised Version); 'Moses wrote' (Mk 12:19); 'Isaiah ... prophesied' (Mk 7:6). Often the reasons for writing demonstrate an ordinary humanity, so that, for example, Luke says that he wrote his Gospel 'because it seemed good ... to write an orderly account' (Lk 1:3).

This humanity is seen not only in the Bible's testimony to itself, but also in the very 'phenomenon' of Scripture. There is a human feel to the writings so that the background and interests of the authors come through in them. For example, Luke's interest in people and his more detailed description of illnesses reveal his medical background. Matthew's Gospel reveals an author with a Jewish background and a desire for orderliness of presentation. Thus the language, culture and background of the author's human background come through the pages of Scripture so that Calvin is quite right in describing parts of Scripture as 'rough and common'.[1]

The inspiration of Scriptures through human agencies is further underlined by the way Scripture came into its present canonical form. Luke wrote his Gospel after first-hand historical research, but clearly used Mark's Gospel and other written sources as part of his data. The writers of Chronicles were dependent on earlier literary sources, and some books passed through several editions (Prov 10:1, 24:23, 25:1). All this is a far cry from some 'dictation' theory of inspiration.

2. The divine element is corrupted in its accommodation to the human element

Every theory of the divine inspiration of Scripture must include some idea of accommodation. Calvin said that in Scripture God 'lisped' to men. In other words, he used baby talk to get on our level of comprehension. But many scholars want to suggest that the divine inspiration of Scripture has necessitated not just God's accommodation to the use of human language but also his accommodation to human imperfections and errors. The divine element of Scripture is fundamentally altered and corrupted by the human element. Just as stained-glass windows change the true colour of the light, so the human authors change and 'colour' the truth. The final product reflects the imperfections and limitations of the human authors in terms of their perception of science, ethics and history. There are several variations in this theory of accommodation.

(A) INSPIRATION COMES THROUGH GOD'S ACCOMMODATION TO HUMAN RELIGIOUS INSIGHT

Inspiration in this case is no different from the way a novelist may have insight on the human condition. Champions of this point of view would say that God is using men and women all the time through ordinary means. So Scripture is just an ordinary book through which God accommodates himself to men. Each genre of literature may express truths with profound insight, but these are essentially man's thoughts, and God has accommodated himself to them. Inevitably the record will be patchy and inconsistent.

The trouble with this theory is that it does not fit with Scripture as we find it. For example, what does one make of those passages which claim to be the direct words of God? They do not fit the normal understanding of religious insight. In which case, what did the authors of these passages think that they were doing?

(B) INSPIRATION COMES THROUGH GOD'S ACCOMMODATION TO HUMAN HISTORY

There are some scholars who gladly accept that God has been at work in history and that he is supremely seen in Christ. However, they would suggest that no special inspiration is needed to record these events. God has already accommodated himself to man through a revelation in human history. The Bible is merely a human document witnessing to divine acts. As such it is full of human fallibilities and its religious worth is patchy.

The problem with this point of view is that Scripture is not just a record of God's revelation in history. There is much exhortation and teaching based on the premise that this is the expression of God's will. Moreover, where history is recorded it is also interpreted so that theology and history are inseparably intertwined. The Bible clearly sees itself as a divine interpretation of history, not just a human record of divine events.

3. The divine element transcends the human element in illumination, not inspiration

Karl Barth's solution to the problem of inspiration was to switch attention from the authors of Scripture to the reader of Scripture. He makes us look not to the mechanics of inspiration, and all its attendant problems, but to the experience of illumination as we now read Scripture. Barth says that, regardless of what Scripture is in itself, we know that it 'becomes' the word of God.

Barth would emphasise the human element in Scripture. The way the Bible was put together would be like any other book. What is different about Scripture, says Barth, is its unique witness to God's revelation in Jesus Christ. However, since God is greater than any book, we must not suggest that we can capture him by some theory of past inspiration. Rather, says Barth, in the present Scripture 'becomes' the word of God as the Holy Spirit opens Scripture to us and makes it the inspired word.

The value of Barth is his emphasis on the dynamic ministry of the Holy Spirit who works today. Without this emphasis, any theory of inspiration will become mechanical. Moreover, there may creep in the subtle temptation to imprison God within our own systems – even though they seem to be based on Scripture. Barth is right to emphasise that God cannot be captured in the past, but is active and speaking now.

The weakness of Barth's point of view is that by emphasising present illumination, he seems to deny past inspiration. Howard Marshall comments: 'illumination now' tends to deny 'inspiration then'.[2] The Bible affirms that what the Spirit did in the past, he can be active doing now. Thus there is a complementarity between the Spirit's work of inspiration and his work of illumination. Barth's doctrine of the Spirit's work in Scripture, therefore, seems to be inconsistent and inadequate.

4. The divine and human elements work together

The traditional position of the Reformers, which evangelicals have sought to espouse, is that Scripture is a truly human document, and yet at the same time it is the utterly reliable word of God. This point of view is sometimes called 'concursive inspiration'. The idea conveyed in this theory is that human efforts are always working together with, and superintended by, God's power. Thus from a human point of view, the Bible is made up like many other human books. The personality of the authors shines through their writing, and their material is sometimes edited, collected and adapted. Yet from a divine point of view, all this is within the purpose and direction of God.

The theory of concursive inspiration therefore demands that we look at Scripture at two complementary levels. This is not something unusual in our Christian experience. For example, when we think of creation we can view it on the scientific level of cause and effect. At the same time we can see creation from a theological angle and acknowledge that behind the world of cause and effect there is a creator. One perspective does not deny the other. This theory of inspiration does not explain the mechanics of inspiration. We are confronted again with a mystery, but the use of analogies reveals that we cannot understand these things in isolation from faith. For example, by faith the Christian expects the sanctifying power of the Spirit to work with our human will. In Christ, of course, we see the ultimate analogy, and the supreme article of faith. He is fully man, yet fully God; both natures working concursively. Again our understanding of the nature of Scripture centres upon the person of Christ.

The implications of concursive inspiration

A century ago, an affirmation of the inspiration of Scripture would have been synonymous with an affirmation of its total reliability and truth. However, the word 'inspiration' has become like a piece of soap. We have tried to grasp it in our discussion above, but have come up with at least four different perspectives. For our purposes now we shall concentrate only on the implications of concursive inspiration. Even here, however, the implications of this doctrine are difficult to grasp. One reason for this has to do with our methodology of study.

Methodology

The results of any doctrine of inspiration will depend, it is argued, on whether we adopt an inductive or deductive approach to Scripture. In other words, if we come to Scripture with a previously formulated doctrine of total truthfulness in Scripture, then deductively we will prove our point. However, if we approach the question with no prior theory, but simply look at the phenomenon of Scripture, then it is argued we would not end with a doctrine of total truthfulness or reliability. We would have to concede that there was error. Someone like James Barr pours scorn on evangelicals who say they take the Bible seriously, but in fact do not. He says they do not take Scripture for what it is, but imprison it within their own restricted formulae. The point at issue is this: do those who accept the claims of Scripture to truth also allow the phenomenon of Scripture itself to speak? How does the inductive approach relate to the deductive approach? Even when committed to a doctrine of concursive inspiration, this methodological question is relevant for it causes differences of opinion among evangelicals.

An historical survey by R C Sproul has shown that the great defenders of the complete truthfulness of Scripture have used both inductive and deductive approaches.[3] The accusation that evangelical scholars have their heads in the sand and will not face the phenomenon of Scripture is just not true. In fact it is noteworthy that in all branches of enquiry, both scientific and theological, there is an informal and two-way relationship between the deductive and inductive approach. Nevertheless, it is important to note that in theology there will always be a priority given to deduction. For example, we could ask the question, 'Was Jesus of Nazareth sinless?' If we began inductively and simply looked at the evidence of his life, any answer would be inadequate. Alternatively, if we began deductively with a doctrine of the sinlessness of Christ, and then tested that theory with the evidence in the New Testament, we would find ourselves on much firmer ground. This methodological order is the approach we ought to adopt.

What does Scripture say about its own truthfulness?

(I) SCRIPTURE AFFIRMS THAT ALL ITS WORDS ARE SPOKEN BY GOD (VERBAL AND PLENARY INSPIRATION)

There are clearly many types of literature, but the Bible does not make a distinction between those passages which are inspired and not inspired. It is easy to see Scripture's claim for those passages where there is direct speech by God to men (at Sinai), or where God's words are spoken by men (prophetic passages). But Scripture goes further in its claim for itself.

Psalm 12:6 says, 'The words of the Lord are pure words' (Authorised Version). This verse, like many others, makes a claim that even narrative and history are still 'the words of the Lord'.

(II) SCRIPTURE AFFIRMS THAT IT IS ALL TRUSTWORTHY AND RELIABLE

Scripture does not suggest that it is only reliable in parts, or that it is only true in a general sense. Very often Scripture quotes Scripture and the argument turns on the minutiae of words. Sometimes a single word is important (Mt 22:43–45; Jn 10:34–35). Sometimes the tense of the verb is significant (Mt 22:32), or the issue turns on whether the word is singular or plural (Gal 3:16). As the word of God, it takes on God's attributes of truthfulness and immutability (Num 23:19; 1 Sam 15:29). Thus, Jesus himself affirms the truthfulness of Scripture saying, 'The

Scripture cannot be broken' (Jn 10:35, see also Mt 5:17–20).

By tying Scripture to the character of God, the Bible is setting its truthfulness apart from any other sort of truthfulness in literature. For example, most human authors can unwittingly make mistakes in what they write. But if they make one error, this does not invalidate everything else they have written. This is not the case with Scripture. The Bible says that it is uniquely God's word to us and that because it is owned and inspired by God it is entirely trustworthy. This doctrine does not come from some isolated proof texts but is backed up, in the words of Warfield, by an avalanche of evidence.

It must be seen from all this evidence that any statement of truthfulness and reliability can first be deduced from scriptural data. To say that the Bible is reliable and truthful is not a position imposed by some cranks, nor is it some recent invention. It is what the Bible says of itself and what Jesus teaches. Having arrived at this doctrine inductively, we can turn to Scripture and see how this understanding can be applied. Our method is deductive (we come with a specific view of Scripture in mind), and yet we hope to be sensitive to the phenomenon of Scripture. What does it mean to say that Scripture is completely truthful and reliable?

The scope of Scripture's truthfulness

The issue of truthfulness is not simple. Strictly speaking, only statements of fact can be given a label of true or false. Thus we can make a considered judgement about the veracity of the fact 'Jesus was born in Bethlehem'. However, we cannot judge in quite the same way Jesus' statement that he is the bread of life. The latter may be true, just as the parables and the Psalms may be true. Yet these are all expressing truth in different forms. Any doctrine concerning the reliability and truthfulness of Scripture must take into account the form in which we find truth. Here are some of the considerations.

(I) TRUTHFULNESS AND LANGUAGE

We know that witnesses giving evidence in court can tell the truth regardless of the correctness of their language. They may have the wrong syntax and grammar, but it does not in any way affect the truth. So in Scripture such considerations of grammar, spelling and syntax do not affect the truth one whit.

In a similar vein, figures of speech do not affect truthfulness. The Psalmist says that the 'rivers clap their hands' and 'the mountains sing together for joy' (Ps 98:8). The language of poetry is such that metaphor and hyperbole are often used. But such figures of speech are not confined to poetry; we find hyperbole in the teaching of Jesus (Mt 5:29). Every literary genre has its peculiarities of style which affect the way we understand truth. For example, apocalyptic literature has to be understood as a literary cartoon, with word pictures that make no literal sense, and yet powerfully convey truth. Moreover, since apocalyptic literature has no parallel today, we need to understand what it meant to write in the genre at that time. We cannot judge the truthfulness of a passage without carefully examining the type of literature and its contemporary usage. Each genre of biblical literature has to be understood in its own terms, whether it is history, poetry, narrative or apocalyptic.

We have begun to see that language has many facets and is closely tied to culture. Language is not just about the arrangement of words, but it is about ideas and values. Thus although we may communicate in the same national language of English, we may still speak unintelligible 'scientific language' or 'accountancy language'. All these sub-languages are dynamic, and with the passing of the years, terms and ideas are superseded by more refined ideas or completely new ones. So it is with the description of the physical world in Scripture. We may wonder at the Bible's phenomenological language describing the universe, but it is merely a different language. Even our present way of describing things is likely to change!

(II) TRUTHFULNESS AND PRECISION

We have already seen that to understand Scripture we have to enter into the experience and intention of the writer in his contemporary situation. We cannot judge grammar or style according to late twentieth-century Western culture. So it is with the issue of precision. Indeed, even today we are aware that precision has different contexts. We would not expect a housewife to be precise about the four minutes it takes to boil an egg, but we would expect the Olympic miler to be precise to a hundredth of a second. So, in biblical literature in some contexts, precision is not very important to the writer. Sometimes we find in accounts of the same incident that one writer is more precise than the other (compare 2 Samuel 10:18 with 1 Chronicles 19:18; compare Matthew 28:5 with Luke 24:4). The result is that we have differences of numbers which represent degrees of precision, but not degrees of truth.

Precision is also an issue when we examine the way the New Testament quotes the Old Testament. From the perspective of late twentieth-century Western culture we want to demand precision, because it is so important in our literature. Again, we have to put ourselves in the position of New Testament authors. They did not have a handy Old Testament to refer to; most of them would be quoting from memory and making a translation at the same time. Moreover, this problem of not having a reference to hand would be a problem to any writer at the time, sacred or secular. So we can safely conclude that in New Testament times the free quotations of other sources were perfectly acceptable and that such quotations still conveyed truth.

Different expectations are also made with regard to precision in speeches. Today we are used to news reporting with tape recording and television. Precision in the reporting of direct speech is axiomatic to accurate research and good reporting. Two thousand years ago these facilities of precise reporting were not available. In all forms of literature it was understood that in the reporting of speeches the meaning should be carefully conveyed even if the exact words were not always used. Now, it is very likely that in many cases we have the *ipsissima verba* (actual words) of Jesus, for he must have often repeated memorable sayings, and someone like Matthew may even have written them down at the time. But not everything would have had such precision. Some of the words of Jesus represent the *ipsissima vox* (actual voice). This explains some of the variety in reporting seen in the Synoptics. All this represents different levels of precision, but not different levels of truthfulness.

(III) TRUTHFULNESS AND PURPOSE

The purpose of a piece of writing has a direct bearing on truth. For example, a newspaper may give a report of a court case in which one witness spins a web of lies. The journalist may have reported faithfully, but what he writes may not be truth, but lies. So Scripture reports things that truly happen, but which may not be true in a moral or theological sense. For example, Job's friends give him bad advice, but Scripture makes no comment on it. Similarly, the imprecatory Psalms speak of the poet's desire for revenge with no comment as to its propriety. In these cases Scripture is 'descriptive' but not 'normative'. Scripture is therefore true in what it 'affirms'.

Some scholars have taken this idea of purpose and intention too far. They would say that the purpose of Scripture is to assist faith and guide living. They therefore limit Scripture merely to matters of faith and practice. However, Scripture does not limit its authority to these areas alone. We may have to recognise the form of phenomenological language about the physical world, and we have to be aware that narrative is not always normative. Nevertheless, we should be able to say that Scripture is true not only in what it affirms, but also in areas it touches.

(IV) TRUTHFULNESS AND PROGRESSION

Any understanding of the truthfulness of Scripture must also take into account some progression in revelation. The most obvious example of progression is the resurrection. In the Old Testament there are few hints of a resurrection life. The New Testament therefore fills out what is incomplete under the old covenant and speaks unmistakably about life eternal with God. This does not contradict previous revelation, nor does it make earlier revelation untrue. There is merely a sense of progression in God's word.

For this reason we can look at the food laws and sacrifices of the Old Testament and see them as true but out of date. The New Testament tells us that these laws are not for us (Acts 10:15; Mk 7:19).

(V) TRUTHFULNESS AND THE INTERPRETATION OF PRESENT DOCUMENTS

One of the most fearful religious phenomena today is the rise of cults. They usually have highly orthodox views of Scripture yet heterodox interpretations. Indeed, the Jehovah's Witnesses would stress the entire truthfulness of Scripture. Thus we must state that the truth of the text still needs faithful and honest handling by the reader. This side of heaven we do not have a finally authoritative interpretation of the text.

Not only do we lack a definitive interpretation of the text, we also lack a definitive text. Some copying errors have slipped into the texts since they were originally written. But our understanding of major doctrines is not in any way affected by these manuscript problems. Nevertheless, it must be stated that only the autograph versions are actually totally reliable and trustworthy.

Shibboleths of truthfulness

In America, the doctrine of Scripture has become a battle-ground. It has caused hurt and schism, especially among Southern Baptists. The reason is that a doctrine of the entire trustworthiness and reliability of Scripture is important and worth fighting for. If we cease to grasp this truth we fail to have authority. Authority is the key issue in society and in the church.

Despite the importance of the issues involved, it is clear that there is a lot of misunderstanding in the debate about the nature of Scripture. Words are used as shibboleths, but they are not defined, so protagonists box with shadows. Very often new words are suggested to define doctrines, but they merely become slogans which create conflicts, not clarity. Moreover, it seems that with some of the slogans there is a danger of oversimplification and false antitheses.

Whatever the slogan, the issue is this: Scripture presents itself to us as being divinely inspired. It claims to be utterly truthful and reliable. As such it is our authority.

Notes

1 John Calvin, *Institutes of the Christian Religion*, Vol I, No viii, p 1.
2 I Howard Marshall, *Biblical Inspiration* (Hodder and Stoughton: London, 1982), p 37.
3 R C Sproul, 'The Case for Inerrancy: a Methodological Analysis' in John Montgomery, ed, *God's Inerrant Word* (Bethany: Minneapolis, MN, 1973), pp 242–61.

4

Interpretation

Today the science of interpretation – hermeneutics – is regarded by many scholars as the key to the question of biblical authority. The history of the church bears this out: so often controversies have arisen not because of a disputed text, but because of a disputed interpretation of a text.

Among scholars today, the way Scripture came together, its structure, date and authorship, greatly affect its interpretation. There are some who will conclude that Scripture has more to tell us about the biblical authors and their cultural context than it has to tell us about the actual events described. Clearly such scepticism about the nature of Scripture affects one's view of its meaning and application. Still other scholars conclude that the problems of interpretation do not centre around the intentions of the original authors, but around the readers of today. Because there is such a dynamic relationship between the reader and his text, some would argue, there can never be a final and authoritative interpretation of Scripture.

Most Christians will want to find a way of interpreting Scripture which is reliable and therefore authoritative. But in order to do this, we need first to see some of the problems posed by scholars down the centuries. Only then can we be constructive about proper methods of interpretation today.

Theories of interpretation up to the Reformation

From the earliest centuries, Christian exegetes have interpreted Scripture from their own philosophic and theological position, together with free allegorisation. Thus although Origen of Alexandria (185–254) did discuss the literal and historical interpretation of Scripture, he always regarded the allegorical understanding as more important. Theodore (350–428) and Chrysostom (337–407) of the Antiochene school were great expositors and more restrained in allegorisation, but the West was to be more influenced by Alexandria than Antioch. In particular, Augustine's method of interpretation dominated the succeeding medieval period. He felt that to be content with a merely literal understanding of the text was to be living a sub-spiritual life, for he would say 'the letter kills, but the Spirit gives life' (2 Cor 3:6). Augustine's method of free allegorisation became a standard form of interpretation for the succeeding centuries.

In the medieval period a fourfold level of interpretation developed and became standard. For example, the word Jerusalem would have four meanings. Literally it was a place, but the moral sense indicated purity; its allegorical meaning was to be seen in a doctrine of the church, and its spiritual meaning was that of the heavenly city. Because of the obscurity of interpretations, great compilations of interpretation were made, like the *Glossa Ordinaria* and the *Magna Glossatura*. Ironically hermeneutical methods became the chief agent of obscurity, not clarity, in the medieval church. Because the Bible could not be interpreted properly, it had no power.

The Reformation, therefore, brought a whirlwind of change. Both Luther and Calvin dismissed allegorisation unequivocally. Luther said, 'We must keep to the simple, pure and natural sense of the words, as demanded by grammar and the use of language created by God among men.' Only where Scripture itself pointed unmistakably to a figurative interpretation was a literal interpretation to be abandoned. From this a grammatico-historical method of interpretation was developed by the Reformers. Any passage had to be understood according to the original meaning of the text; with due consideration to the language used, the genre of literature and the historical and cultural context. Moreover, the Reformers saw that the Scriptures must be their own interpreter, and not shackled by another authority, even that of the church. All this interpretive method was to be guided by the Spirit, who alone gave true understanding of the word. These hermeneutical methods stand today and are discussed again below.

Modern theories of interpretation

The Reformation provided a new foundation for biblical study. Consistent with the grammatico-historical method, scholars began to study the text itself in order to find that which is authentic. This textual study was called 'lower criticism'. Thus, for example, J J Wettstein (1693–1754) published a two-volume Greek New Testament with a text that departed from the Textus Receptus. Other works drew attention to variant texts in the Greek, so J A Bengel (1687–1752) classified these different witnesses to the text. He provided the rule 'the difficult reading is to be preferred to the easy one'.

By the nineteenth century, scholarly interest turned not just to the text of Scripture, but to the literary form in which we find it. 'Higher criticism' tried to analyse the structure, date and authorship of the different biblical books. W M L De Wette (1780–1849) gave a theory of the composition of the Pentateuch and saw in the New Testament three different theological strands: Jewish/Christian, Alexandrian and Pauline. Karl Lachmann (1793–1851), in addition to remarkable work on the Greek text, also pioneered the way to an acceptance of Markan priority among the Gospels. Ferdinand Baur (1762–1860), the leader of the 'Tübingen School', declared that only Romans, Galatians and the Corinthian letters were genuinely Pauline. The Gospels were all written in the first century, according to Baur, and John's Gospel was written in the second half of the second century.

The rationalism of the age, coupled with the result of both 'lower' and 'higher' criticism, led nineteenth-century scholars to sceptical interpretations of Scripture. For example, Friedrich Schleiermacher (1768–1834) reinterpreted the supernatural elements of the Gospels entirely in terms of rational possibility and proven observable phenomena. David Friedrich Strauss (1808–1874) went much further. He took it as axiomatic that the transcendent God could not be involved in the affairs of men. The Gospels were therefore to be interpreted, not rationalistically, but mythologically. Albert Schweitzer (1875–1965) made the logical conclusion from all this liberal scholarship that we can know almost nothing about the real historical Jesus.

With such uncertainty about the nature and form of the text, it is not surprising that there could be no authoritative interpretation of Scripture. The grammatico-historical method seemed to lead to an impasse. For this reason a new hermeneutic was sought beyond the minutiae of the actual text. If principal themes could be discovered, then interpreting Scripture would be just applying these overriding motifs; retaining the kernel of truth and discarding all the husks. Thus many suggestions have been made about the overriding forms or themes of Scripture.

Alternative interpretations

New foci within the subject of Scripture

(I) ESCHATOLOGY

Schweitzer suggested that the New Testament should be reinterpreted with a deeper understanding of the eschatological element. Jesus, he said, was an apocalyptic figure who threw himself into the wheel of history in order to precipitate the coming of a kingdom which was always in the future. Later Rudolf Otto and C H Dodd demonstrated that the kingdom was not just future, but present. Their studies provided a new focus of understanding by many other scholars. Jesus is both the fulfiller of past promises and the Amen to what lies ahead.

(II) 'SALVATION HISTORY' (HEILSGESCHICHTE)

Another school of thought has suggested that the Bible is to be regarded primarily as a record of salvation history. The term was first coined by J T Beck in the eighteenth century, but more recently Oscar Cullmann has revived the idea. By this method of interpretation the Bible is delivered from being just an ordinary history book. Rather it is seen as a testimony to an increasing awareness of God's saving work in history. As such it confronts the believer in the present with a God who is active and relevant.

New foci within the writing of Scripture

(III) 'HISTORY OF RELIGION' (RELIGIONSGESCHICHTE)

This school of thought attempted to put the witness of the early Christians into their own cultural and religious context. For example, Reizenstein sees an Iranian redemption myth as a tool for interpreting the New Testament. Later Bultmann would attempt to reinterpret the New Testament as though it were all in the form of a Jewish and Hellenist myth. The hermeneutical task of the reader is therefore to discern the myth, and peer through this to the *kerygma*.

(IV) 'LIFE SITUATION'

Another hermeneutical principle, championed by scholars like Hans Conzelmann, has been to discern the church situation at the time when the New Testament letters and Gospels were written. Thus, the effect of the post-apostolic era and the concerns of a church adjusting to a delayed *parousia*, and institutionalised ministry, have all to be discerned. Again, the hermeneutical task is to understand the life situation of the church and then to reinterpret the meaning of the text.

(V) THE ROLE OF THE REDACTOR

Just as some scholars have sought to find out the life situation of the church, still others have tried to work out the background to the authors themselves. Of course, the two are closely related but provide yet another way of interpretation.

New foci within the reading of Scripture

(VI) THE EXISTENTIAL

The appeal to history on the basis of Scripture has been, for many, a doubtful task. Bultmann would suggest that the task is irrelevant anyway. Just as Paul did not want to know Jesus 'after the flesh' (2 Cor 5:16, Authorised Version), so we do not need history. All that is important is an existential encounter with Jesus, regardless of any truth or untruth about the historical Jesus.

(VII) THE NEW HERMENEUTIC

Bultmann's existential approach was undoubtedly a stimulus for the 'new hermeneutic' which was propounded by his disciples. Bultmann always maintained that the study of Scripture could never be purely detached and objective but that there was a dialogue between the object and subject of knowledge. Bultmann's ideas originate with Martin Heidegger (1889–1976) and lead to the idea of a 'hermeneutical circle'. This means that the interpreter is himself interpreted by Scripture, so that he comes back to Scripture with new eyes. Thus, through reading Scripture, we can know the text (*wissen*), but only through interaction with the text can we actually understand the text (*verstehen*).

E Fuchs and G Ebeling go further than Bultmann and suggest that the meaning of the text is buried in the process of speech itself. So, when the word of God is proclaimed there is a 'language occurrence' (*Sprachereignis*) or 'word event' (*Wortgeschehen*). In this existential event, God's saving action comes into the present and brings faith.

An evaluation of these approaches

These approaches reveal a scepticism which reflects the spirit of the age

George Tyrrell once described the Jesus Christ presented in the work of Adolf Harnack as 'the reflection of a Liberal Protestant face, seen at the bottom of a deep well'. Here we must agree with Bultmann, there is no such thing as 'presuppositionless' exegesis, for every age and every personality brings spectacles coloured by that age. Thus the extreme scepticism of the nineteenth century is the result of its commitment to rationalism. If those rationalistic principles are proved wrong then their conclusions are suspect.

For example, why should the supernatural and miraculous be automatically excluded or explained away from Scripture? Do we have to believe that our world is a closed system into which the transcendent God cannot break? If this is the case, then God ceases to be God. The fundamental principle of incarnation, that the eternal Word did become flesh, has to be abandoned at a stroke. If, however, we do believe in Jesus as the incarnate Word, we are already committed to God's supernatural action in the world.

The extreme scepticism of higher and lower criticism is just a reflection of the extreme rationalism of the nineteenth century. However, the legacy of this spirit is alive today. For example, presuppositions about the phenomenon of Scripture, its historical accuracy and literary form, have led to many of the sceptical approaches outlined below. James Barr sees Scripture as a 'pluriform, multilayered testament of religious experience [and/or] insight which testifies unevenly and fallibly to the God we experience'.[1] Yet again the human mind is trying to grapple with Scripture in familiar categories without an openness to a supernatural dimension. There are vast tracts of research in parallel forms of contemporary literature, and yet Scripture as a whole defies categorisation. Some of its genre of literature remain unique. For example, to what genre of contemporary literature could one compare a Gospel? The phenomenological approach simply cannot answer all the questions. There is a uniqueness to Scripture which goes beyond a merely rationalistic approach.

The 'history of religions' approach is therefore merely looking for types of literature outside of Scripture which, it is assumed, will have a parallel within the biblical canon. The search for the church 'life situation' is again based on assumptions about the genesis of biblical literature without any concession to the fact that God may be at work superintending his work. In fact, each of the alternative interpretive methods above can be viewed as a merely rationalistic explanation of Scripture. As such they are inadequate.

These approaches are far too subjective

In any science the selection of evidence to back up a thesis is of crucial importance. Thus the methodology of any investigation needs careful testing lest the researcher's own selectivity colour the evidence. Unfortunately for the biblical scholar, the evidence – Scripture itself – is a finite and relatively small area of research. Moreover a thesis cannot be tested by repetition and experiment as in a laboratory. All these factors make biblical research difficult. Theories can be based on slender evidence, and the hypotheses are difficult to test.

Recent study has shown that many of the conclusions made by the 'history of religions' have a tenuous basis. For example, Bultmann suggested that parts of the New Testament have a Gnostic background, and that the second-century Redeemer myth of the Gnostics can be seen in the New Testament. However, there is no evidence that this myth existed in pre-Christian times. Moreover, there is a circularity of argument. It is first suggested that there is a Gnostic background, and then the New Testament is used as the main source for defining the type of Gnosticism that was prevalent.

The same sort of subjectivity influences the other alternative theories of interpretation. For example, the 'life situation' in which a Gospel story is born is based on the evidence found in the text. If there is a reference to bread in the narrative it is assumed that this reflects the early church's preoccupation with the Eucharist. If there is a reference to water, it is because the early church is concerned with baptism. But one could also say that bread and water were integral parts of the original story and did not need to be invented by the church.

Subjectivity can be at its worst in the New Hermeneutic. Clark Pinnock writes, 'The text is in motion. It stands in dynamic existential relationship with its interpreter, and may be interpreted in the opposite way from that which the writer intended.'[2] Although there are so many good things to learn from the New Hermeneutic, if the existential element of personal encounter is exalted above a desire for some objective truth, then we will be lost in a mire of subjectivity.

These approaches cannot be used exclusively

Most of the alternative hermeneutics mentioned above have some useful insights which can help in the interpretation of Scripture. The chaff of each theory has to be blown away, and the kernel of truth applied judiciously.

Above all, no one theory can be used to the exclusion of the others. Thus the suggestion that one subject, like eschatology or salvation, holds the key to all else in Scripture is unhelpful. Similarly, to concentrate merely on the life situation of the early church or on the mind-set of the original author is to have too narrow a perspective. Each suggestion must be weighed carefully as to its value and interpreted in a wider hermeneutical framework. Some indication of this framework is indicated below.

An evangelical approach to interpretation

Without clear principles of biblical interpretation, a high doctrine of inspiration is merely academic. Like saying 'abracadabra', everything becomes uncertain with the magic word 'hermeneutics'. Scholars and laymen alike are tempted to get out of a tight spot by saying, 'Well, of course it is all a matter of interpretation.' This dishonesty can only be stopped by a carefully thought out method of biblical interpretation.

The search for this hermeneutic is not easy, and will never be complete. For the word of God does not lie down like a dead dog to be analysed and cut up. Rather, it is 'living and active' (Heb 4:12), and is always interpreting and challenging the reader like a live 'double-edged sword' (Heb 4:12). A hermeneutic is needed which brings objectivity to that part of the study of Scripture which is like the dissecting table; but in those areas where Scripture addresses us personally and dynamically our method must have a form which restrains wild speculation and encourages objectivity.

Most of the principles outlined below were first enunciated at the time of the Reformation. It is no surprise to see that although every age has its hermeneutical challenge, many of the essential problems of interpretation remain the same. For the medieval reader the search for the 'deeper' allegorical meaning meant that the original intention of the biblical authors and the meaning to contemporary readers was often not taken seriously. A similar desire to side-step the original meaning of the text is to be found today. An existential approach will cheerfully demythologise the text because, they say, what matters is that God speaks now. Thus the hermeneutical principles of the Reformers have great value today. However, the dynamic nature of Scripture was not such an issue in the sixteenth century as it is today in the twentieth century. The method outlined below is an attempt to take Reformation principles and apply them to a present-day, more dynamic, understanding of Scripture.

Step 1: exegesis – what does the passage actually say?

The first great Reformation principle of interpretation is that the natural or literal understanding of the text must be the foundation for all further study. Today this method is called the grammatico-historical method. It is essentially an exercise in understanding the text from the point of view of the original author and those who would have first read the documents. Thus modern values and presuppositions are not to be read into the ancient text, but the text stands in its own time and culture. Thus, questions must be asked of the text.

(I) WHAT DID THE TEXT SAY IN ITS ORIGINAL LANGUAGE?

The study of biblical languages, their grammar and syntax, can yield subtleties of understanding that are quite significant. For example, some may think it is important that in Genesis 1 the Hebrew term translated as 'day' can also be translated as 'age'.

(II) WHAT DID THE TEXT SAY IN ITS ORIGINAL LITERARY GENRE?

The Bible is a library of different types of literature which includes history, poetry, narrative and parable. Each genre needs to be understood in its contemporary literary context. For example, there is no modern parallel for apocalyptic. Unless one appreciates that it is meant to be viewed like a modern-day cartoon one will be lost in the bizarre imagery. Similarly, to understand genealogies in the Bible one needs to appreciate the significance of that genre in the ancient world. It was not to present every single forebear without exception, but often only to show the important people in that line. To do this was not being inaccurate, as we might judge today, but rather it was being true to a literary form.

(III) WHAT DID THE TEXT SAY IN ITS ORIGINAL CULTURE?

The Bible is full of images and expressions which are unintelligible in our culture. For example, what does it mean to 'heap burning coals upon his head' or to say 'Raca' or to 'shake the dust off your feet'? A superficial answer with no knowledge of the cultural context will give, not just an inadequate answer, but possibly a completely wrong one. So, archaeology and contemporary literary studies will enable us to understand the background of the Bible and so enrich our understanding of Scripture today.

(IV) WHAT DID THE AUTHOR INTEND THE TEXT TO SAY?

Every writer has his reader in mind. The historian with a theological purpose in mind may ignore, therefore, the major economic achievements of a reign. Instead he may feel it is the spiritual significance of a king that is the most important aspect to be recorded. Thus the expectations of modern comprehensive history simply do not apply to books like Chronicles. The author's intention also colours the way we will understand the ultimate meaning of a text. For example, in matters of religion and moral life the Corinthian church and the Galatian church represent opposites. The former were antinomian, whereas the latter were bound by legalism. The same author, Paul, tackles similar issues but from diametrically opposed positions. To fail to understand the intention of the author would be to suggest that Paul was confused.

Step 2: synthesis – what does the passage mean?

To understand the meaning of an individual text, one needs to go beyond the grammatico-historical method and put it in the context of the whole of Scripture. This is called harmonisation and is a practice derived from the belief that Scripture has a single author and therefore a unity. The Reformers put it simply: Scripture is its own interpreter. This principle has several implications.

(I) WE MUST INTERPRET SCRIPTURE BY SCRIPTURE; THE OBSCURE BY THE PLAIN

The Bible is a book with many echoes. Themes run from Genesis to Revelation, but each passage has a different nuance. Allowing one part to interpret the other brings clarity, particularly where the meaning is obscure. Thus, for example, the book of Revelation is made clear by reference to Old Testament imagery.

(II) WE MUST INTERPRET SCRIPTURE BY SCRIPTURE; THE EARLIER IN THE LIGHT OF THE LATER

Unlike an echo of sound which gets quieter and more diffuse, the echoes of Scripture become louder and more clear. This is known as progressive revelation. This does not imply, however, that one part of Scripture corrects another but rather that later Scripture explains and fills out what went before. Thus the Old Testament is to be understood in the light of the New. So, Jesus says that he 'fulfils the law', yet at the same time upholds its abiding quality (Mt 5:17).

(III) WE MUST INTERPRET SCRIPTURE BY ITS OWN INTENTION

Paul explains that the purpose of Scripture is to make the man of God 'thoroughly equipped for every good work' (2 Tim 3:16). In other words, Scripture's main intention is not to be a textbook on science, history or geography, but a guide to the things of God. When it touches on matters concerning the physical world, it does so truthfully in the terms of the age. However, to explain science is not Scripture's intention, and that purpose should not be foisted onto it.

(IV) WE MUST INTERPRET SCRIPTURE BY ITS OWN HERMENEUTIC

Because Scripture refers to itself so often, there is an implicit method of interpreting itself. Thus many of the hermeneutical principles already outlined are drawn from Scripture's own method. For example, Scripture sees itself as a unity and as having divine authority. But perhaps the most problematic hermeneutical principle is the way the New Testament quotes and interprets the Old Testament. The argument goes like this: since the New Testament authors quoted so freely as in the Rabbinic mode, we too are free to be inexact with the text and not to be too burdened with exact words. It is suggested that the New Testament's own hermeneutic is very free and imprecise – a far cry from any doctrine of verbal inspiration.

This supposition concerning a free hermeneutic is quite wrong. It is clear that whenever the New Testament authors quote the Old Testament they do so to a largely Jewish readership who were already familiar with the exact text. Thus the New Testament authors were not debating precise details of text, but the sense of the passage. In a similar way we might paraphrase a passage to make a point. Although there are examples where the New Testament quotes the Old Testament without exact precision, there are also examples where the argument turns on one word or one letter. Indeed, Jesus speaks of the importance of 'the smallest letter and the least stroke of the pen' (Mt 5:15). In other words, the Bible takes its own words seriously.

Step 3: application – what is the significance of this passage for today?

MEANING AND SIGNIFICANCE

So far we have been asking the questions 'What does the text say and mean?' There can be considerable objectivity in this pursuit. What the original author meant when he wrote a particular passage can be evaluated and tested according to the grammatico-historical method. There is a subject-object relationship between the reader and the text. However, when we ask, 'What is the significance of the text?' there is a new dynamic between the reader and his text. The reader himself becomes the object of interpretation as the word questions him. Although some scholars have taken this process too far, there are nevertheless two important reasons why the process is valid.

First, our fallen minds require the illumination and correction of the Holy Spirit. It would be possible to allow the interpretation of Scripture to be ruled by rationalistic methods as though these in themselves revealed truth. But the Bible indicates that insights into truth only come from God. Thus Jesus perceives that God himself had opened Peter's eyes when he makes his confession at Caesarea Philippi (Mt 16:17). Later in his ministry Jesus explains the role of the Holy Spirit who will 'teach you all things' (Jn 14:26). We therefore cannot assume that we will understand Scripture – either its meaning or significance – without the Spirit's illumination. The Christian reader does not have a merely subject-object relationship with the text: there is a third party involved interpreting both!

The dynamic nature of Scripture is the second reason why there can be no simple subject-object relation in interpreting it. Unlike any other book, there is a life to Scripture which operates independently of the reader. Whether we like it or not, whether we want it or not, Scripture comes like a sword to interpret us. We do not control Scripture by our clever methods; rather, Scripture seeks to control and direct us. There has to be a dynamic approach to the interpretation of Scripture.

THE HERMENEUTICAL CIRCLE

Recently scholars have described the dynamic of interpretation in terms of a circle, or dialogue, between the interpreter and his text. As we have already seen, the text itself needs to be opened by proper questions. For example, we will ask, 'What is the linguistic and historical context of the passage? What did the original author intend to say, and what does that mean in the context of the whole of Scripture?' But then we may find that the passage itself begins to speak to us in our situation. It may question existing assumptions about our worldview. The preconceptions of our culture, time and tradition are sifted by Scripture. It is as though we are given clearer spectacles with which to see Scripture. Thus we come back to Scripture with different questions but clearer insight. The Holy Spirit allows Scripture to do its work, 'it [Scripture] penetrates even to dividing soul and spirit, joints and marrow; it judges the thoughts and attitudes of the heart' (Heb 4:12).

Anthony Thiselton comments:

> The 'circle' of the hermeneutical process begins when the interpreter takes his own preliminary questions to the text. But because his questions may not be the best or the most appropriate ones, his understanding of the subject-matter of the text may at first remain limited, provisional and even liable to distortion. Nevertheless the text speaks back to the hearer: it begins to interpret him; it sheds light on his own situation and on his own questions. His initial questions now undergo revision in the light of the text itself, and in response to more adequate questioning, the text now speaks more clearly and intelligibly. The process continues, whilst the interpreter achieves a progressively deeper understanding of the text.[3]

Is this a recipe for total uncertainty?

Many evangelicals have felt threatened by the more dynamic element of interpretation, and have wondered whether it makes everything uncertain. Their suspicions have been exacerbated by some scholars who suggest that there can never be a certain and authoritative interpretation. However, there are some important safeguards which prevent interpretation slipping into total subjectivity.

First, the hermeneutical circle is not a circle that turns endlessly, but rather a spiral which leads to a point. Jim

Packer says that this is 'not circles of presuppositions which you ought to prove, but a succession of approximations, a basic method in every science'. So he says, 'We rise from the less exact and well tested understanding to the one that is more so.'[4] In this light we can say that the 'hermeneutical spiral' gives to Scripture still more authority, not less. At last interpretation is released from the idiosyncrasies of private subjectivism to a more exact science.

Secondly, our present interpretation of the Scriptures is made more sure by checking it against the interpretation of godly men in the past. Men and women of other generations have put themselves humbly under the authority of word and Spirit and have provided us with an interpretation. It would be most surprising if the same word and Spirit worked differently in another age. The Holy Spirit may bring insights on truths neglected, forgotten or perverted, but there will always be a consistency in the Spirit's work. So church tradition plays an important supportive role in the interpretation of Scripture. The Bible is never ruled by the church in the sense that there is an official church line. Rather, tradition acts as a bench-mark checking wild extremes and fanciful interpretations.

When can we say, 'Scripture speaks with clarity and authority'?

We can say that Scripture speaks with clarity and authority:

(1) When we have understood what Scripture *says* in its proper linguistic and historical context.

(2) When we have understood what it *means* in the whole context and purpose of Scripture.

(3) When we have understood its *significance* by humbly recognising our own limitations of culture and tradition; and in dependence upon the Holy Spirit, who has guided others in the past, allowed Scripture to interpret us.

Notes

1 James Packer's summary of J Barr in Donald Carson and John Woodbridge, eds, *Scripture and Truth* (Inter Varsity Press: Leicester, 1983), p 353.
2 Clark Pinnock, *Biblical Revelation* (Moody: Chicago, Il, 1971), p 226.
3 Anthony Thiselton, *New Testament Interpretation* (Paternoster: Exeter, 1977), p 316.
4 James Packer's summary *op cit*, p 348.

5

Living under Authority

It is one thing to acknowledge authority; it is another matter to live under it. In fact, a mere acknowledgement of authority without any commitment to it denies the very meaning of authority. For authority is the power or right to command obedience. So if we pick what we choose to obey, then we make ourselves the ultimate arbiter of authority. Supreme authority lies within us.

The story of the centurion is, therefore, a wonderful picture of what it means to live under authority. The centurion says, 'I myself am a man under authority, with soldiers under me. I tell this one, "Go," and he goes; and that one, "Come," and he comes. I say to my servant, "Do this," and he does it' (Mt 8:9). In other words, when you live under authority you do what you are told, with no right to pick or choose the options. If Jesus is our authority and if we believe his will is revealed in Scripture, then we must be like the centurion – people under authority. It does not matter how orthodox our view of Scripture is;

if we fail to live under Scripture's authority, all other discussion is profitless.

Ironically, it is often those who exalt authority who least live under it. Authoritarianism, whether political or religious, uses an 'authority' like a puppeteer uses a doll. The central issue in the authority of Scripture is this: who is master? Do we master Scripture, or does Scripture master us? D A Carson rebukes evangelicals for raping the Bible and doing injustice to it 'for its own good'! 'We have hungered to be masters of the Word much more than we have hungered to be mastered by it.'[1]

The debate about the authority of Scripture is ultimately a debate about practice. It concerns our intention to submit to a will other than our own. The battle is therefore not so much in our minds as in our hearts. The weapons of our warfare are not just words but above all, humility, prayer and action.

Notes

1 Donald Carson, *Hermeneutics, Authority and Canon* (Inter Varsity Press: Leicester, 1986), p 47.